Out of Wonder

CELEBRATING POETS AND POETRY

KWAME ALEXANDER

with **CHRIS COLDERLEY** and **MARJORY WENTWORTH**

ILLUSTRATED BY
EKUA HOLMES

CANDLEWICK PRESS

CONTENTS

PREFACE

Poetry is serious, playful, all-encompassing, specific, divine, incomprehensible, profane.
—*Wynton Marsalis*

My father was a writer, professor, and book publisher. My mother was a school principal and a storyteller who taught English at the local college. Both of my parents loved words the way fire loves air. In my home, words came alive. There were read-alouds before breakfast and poetry theater after dinner. Our house was a Walmart of books. And reading was our hobby, our playdate. When we misbehaved, it was our punishment. While my friends entertained themselves with board games and video games, I turned to books. My shelves were lined with Dr. Seuss, Eloise Greenfield, Lee Bennett Hopkins, and Lucille Clifton's Everett Anderson books. I knew these poets intimately and their books word for word. There was little room in our house for things like television. My siblings and I might catch reruns of *I Love Lucy* or old westerns on a Saturday, but only if my father was traveling.

A poem is a small but powerful thing. It has the power to reach inside of you, to ignite something in you, and to change you in ways you never imagined. There is a feeling of connection and communion—with the author and the subject—when we read a poem that articulates our deepest feelings. That connection can be a vehicle on the road to creativity and imagination. Poems can inspire us—in our classrooms and in our homes—to write our own journeys, to find our own voices.

The title of this book, *Out of Wonder*, comes from a quote by renowned poet and children's book author Lucille Clifton. She wrote, "Poems come out of wonder, not out of knowing." Writers often struggle with the blank page. A clean slate can motivate, but it can also scare us. We are always in search of experiences that spark ideas for our poems and stories. Inspiration can also come from reading the works of other poets. Poems are not static objects.

They are ever-evolving ideas that speak to us in different ways at different times in our lives.

I remember reading and reading lots of poetry in first and second grades. I could barely contain my excitement when I "got" a poem and could explain it to someone else. Sometime between then and high school, poetry, for the most part, vanished from the classroom. What remained was incomprehensible. And that was no fun. Happily, in college I rediscovered the magic of poetry. I don't want you to have to wait that long.

Allow me to introduce you to twenty of my favorite poets. Poets who have inspired me and my co-authors with their words and their lives. They can do the same for you. Some of the poets we celebrate in this book lived centuries ago and wrote in languages other than English, while others still walk the streets of San Antonio and New York City today. Chris Colderley, Marjory Wentworth, and I had two requirements for the poets we would celebrate in *Out of Wonder:* first, they had to be interesting people, and second, we had to be passionately in love with their poetry. *Mission accomplished!*

I believe that by reading other poets we can discover our own wonder. For me, poems have always been muses. The poems in this book pay tribute to the poets being celebrated by adopting their style, extending their ideas, and offering gratitude to their wisdom and inspiration.

Enjoy the poems. We hope to use them as stepping-stones to wonder, leading you to write, to read the works of the poets celebrated in this book, to seek out more about their lives and their work, or to simply read and explore more poetry. At the very least, maybe you can memorize one or two.

We wonder how you will wonder.

— Kwame Alexander

PART I
GOT STYLE?

Poets love to make up their own rules about writing;
that's what makes it so much fun. Sometimes
e. e. cummings and Nikki Giovanni use ellipses (…)
to separate ideas and lowercase letters at the beginning
of sentences. Langston Hughes, who loved jazz, was
a master of repetition, rhythm, rhyming couplets, and
quatrains. The poems in this section pay tribute to
the poets being celebrated by adopting their styles
and rhythms.

HOW TO WRITE A POEM

celebrating Naomi Shihab Nye

Hush.

Grab a pencil
some paper
spunk.

Let loose your heart —
raise your voice.

What if I have many voices?

Let them dance together
twist and turn
like best friends
in a maze
till you find
your way
to that one true word

(or two).

—KWAME ALEXANDER

3

IN EVERY SEASON
celebrating Robert Frost

In every season I have wandered
on paths that wind through fields and woods

beside my farm, marked by low stone walls
strung across the hills like unwound string.

Out beyond the pasture and the brook
bubbling beneath the pines, I have walked

on ice through starless winter nights
into the orchard frozen in moonlight.

I have stopped to shake the dry snow
from the branches and watched the outline

of each bare tree sharpen like stone
and considered that quite often

life is too much like a pathless wood.
Still I have lived so long and traveled far,

and I have climbed these hills and looked
at the world and descended.

— MARJORY WENTWORTH

I LIKE YOUR

celebrating e. e. cummings

I like my shoes when they are with
your shoes. Mostly the comes. Leastly
the goes. I carry your footsteps(onetwothreefour)
in between today(. . .)tomorrow.
Again
      and again
             and again
                    I like
to feel the flowers,and the follow
to your lead.
It is such a happy thing to yes the next with you
to walk on magic love rugs beneath the what
and why nots
the anythings of
liking everybloomingthing — four feet, two hearts, one
great   GREAT   GREAT(US)

going.

—KWAME ALEXANDER

CONTEMPORARY HAIKU
celebrating Bashō

Desks in tidy rows
Notebooks and texts neatly stacked
New year begins soon.

Thunder and lightning
Rain soaking the school blacktop
Recess bells silent.

Pens scratching paper
Syllables counted with care
Poets blossoming.

—CHRIS COLDERLEY

SNAPSHOTS
celebrating Nikki Giovanni

people forget . . . poetry is not just words on a page . . . it is . . .
a snowflake on your tongue . . . a tattoo on the inside of your arm . . . a *dashiki* and a *kaftan* . . .
tripping down the streets of Lincoln Heights . . . shouting from the hills of Knoxville, Tennessee . . .

poetry is . . . barbecue . . . cotton candy . . . purple skin beets from Daddy's garden . . .
blues . . . the Birdland jazz club . . . Sunday morning gospel . . . chasing justice . . . freedom . . .

poetry is remembering the things that matter . . . the ones you love . . .
when night comes softly . . . like ripples on a pond

—CHRIS COLDERLEY

9

JAZZ JIVE JAM

celebrating Langston Hughes

On Saturday, my mama sang
a song that sounded blue.
Then Daddy made his trumpet cry —
I guess the rent is due.

'Round midnight came a band of neighbors
swinging soul to soul.
The landlord even cut a rug
and let the good times roll.

They all ate Mama's waffles and
her chicken Cordon Bleu.
Then Daddy passed his hat around,
because the rent is due.

Come Sunday, me and Mama kneeled
while Deacon Willie prayed.
When we got home, my daddy cheered,
"Hooray, the rent's been paid!"

—KWAME ALEXANDER

PART II

IN YOUR SHOES

Sometimes our poems sound like they were written by our favorite poets, and that is okay. It's easy to incorporate the feelings and themes of the poets we are reading into our own work. Walter Dean Myers loved basketball, Judith Wright was a well-known environmentalist, and Billy Collins makes you laugh out loud with his conversational and witty observations on the everyday happenings of life. Using these ideas, we can create our own masterpieces.

WALTER, AGE TEN
celebrating Walter Dean Myers

I'd like to soar one day
    like Sweetwater Clifton high above the rim —
I wanna trot the globe
    grab the world in my hands and
twirl a big ball of hope
    from corner to corner.
Yeah, Daddy-o, soon as I get me some wings
    I'm gonna name the stars
after my buddies
    put 'em each in a story of their own
so we never forget
    the summers we spent
watching sweeties double Dutch
    stealing pop bottles from Mrs. Lomax
ballin' on the blacktop and
    fightin' our way home after we won.
Yeah, one day I'll stand on my stoop
    look out at all the nurses, the poets
the workers, the hustlers
    and color them my heroes
beautiful and brilliant heroes
    bouncing round here
in Harlem.

—KWAME ALEXANDER

A FIELD OF ROSES

celebrating Emily Dickinson

I keep an old verse in my room
That says believing in roses makes them bloom.
I know enough of life's toil
To say it also takes rich, fertile soil
Lots of good, old-fashioned care
And rain to make roses blossom in air.
Here a beautiful red field grows —
I'd say the loveliest anyone knows.

—CHRIS COLDERLEY

THE BLUE ALPHABET
celebrating Terrance Hayes

Make a paint box out of letters;
add water and dip your brush.
Swirl it on the paper with style
while you are humming a tune,
smiling or standing still. Waiting
for the school bus, you can dazzle
your friends with the words you have
made and strung together
like beads around your neck.

— MARJORY WENTWORTH

HOW BILLY COLLINS WRITES A POEM
celebrating Billy Collins

When you first wake up, notice
how your mother's voice, calling
you to breakfast, sounds like a fire alarm.
Watch the steam rising off your oatmeal
like tiny clouds and guess where it goes.

Pay attention to the smallest things:
a fly buzzing near the kitchen window,
bright rocks in the driveway,
the handful of marbles in your pocket —
the sound they make when you walk.

Imagine that the leaves spinning in the wind
on the walk to school are alien ships
and that barking dogs belong to a prince.
At night, when the stars seem close
reach up and grab some.

Our lives are made from these things,
and when you describe them,
you discover magic. It's the way
your pen becomes a wand in your hand,
and this may be the only thing you need to know.

— MARJORY WENTWORTH

THE MUSIC OF THE EARTH
celebrating Pablo Neruda

No matter how far I traveled —
across glaciers and snow-covered
mountains and roads thick with mud,
from one corner of the world
to another, through years of war
and exile and love, I always
returned to the green silence
of the Chilean forest,
where my words linger
and accumulate like rocks
blurring in the cold rain.

I found a place where the wild
sea beat against the back
of my country. And I stayed,
on Isla Negra, watching
wave upon wave break below
my window, while I sat
at a table inscribing
the language of water —
finding new words for salt
and starlight, describing
how the wind tastes, writing
the struggles of my people.

—MARJORY WENTWORTH

ABOUT THE POETS BEING CELEBRATED

Maya Angelou (1928 – 2014)

Maya Angelou's extraordinary life is a testament to the power of endurance. She was born in a segregated rural area of St. Louis, Missouri, but she spent long periods of time in the rural south with her grandmother in Stamps, Arkansas. Her childhood was particularly difficult, having been abused at the age of seven. In 1940, Angelou moved to San Francisco, where she graduated from high school at sixteen and gave birth to a son at seventeen. She began dancing lessons for a career in theater, and became the city's first female African-American streetcar conductor. She continued acting and performing off and on throughout her life.

Angelou recounts her life as a dancer touring Europe in the cast of *Porgy and Bess* in the third volume of her autobiography, *Singin' and Swingin' and Gettin' Merry Like Christmas*. In the late 1950s, she joined the Harlem Writers Guild and became involved with the American civil rights movement. In the early 1960s, she lived and worked overseas: first in Cairo, then in Ghana, where she was a writer and an editor for the *African Review*. She was among the cast members of the historic television miniseries *Roots* in the late 1970s.

Altogether, Maya Angelou wrote six autobiographies. The first book, *I Know Why the Caged Bird Sings*, became a bestseller. She also wrote several volumes of poetry, including *Oh Pray My Wings Are Going to Fit Me Well* in 1975, *And Still I Rise* in 1978, *I Shall Not Be Moved* in 1990, and *The Complete Collected Poems of Maya Angelou* in 1994. Her poems are admired for their inspirational and motivational messages. In addition, she is the author of several books for children, as well as collections of essays. In 1993, she recited her poem "On the Pulse of Morning" at President Bill Clinton's inauguration.

Over the years, she has received numerous honors and awards, including more than fifty honorary degrees from colleges and universities. She received the National Medal of Arts in 2000, and in 2011 was presented with the Presidential Medal of Freedom. When Maya Angelou passed away in 2014, she received tributes from Oprah Winfrey, President Barack Obama, and former president Clinton, among others.

Bashō (1644 – 1694)

Japanese poet Bashō was born Matsuo Kinksaku in 1644 in a rural village near the city of Kyoto. He was a master practitioner of *renga*, linked verse composed of two- and three-line stanzas, and he was among the first to treat the three-line stanzas, usually of five, seven, and five syllables, as a stand-alone form. These poems are known today as haiku, and Bashō's ideas about the form remain in practice: attention to time and place, precisely observed imagery, a seasonal reference, and the use of ordinary language.

In his late twenties, he moved from Kyoto to Edo, which is now Tokyo, where he became part of the literary community. In 1680, after a student gave him some banana (*bashō*) trees, he began writing under the name Bashō. He also studied Zen Buddhism. He was a prolific traveler, making several months-long journeys throughout his life, and he used those experiences to create a new form called *haibun*, a combination of prose and haiku. His best-known collection of *haibun* is *Oku no Hosomichi*, or *The Narrow Road to the Interior*. It recounts a twelve-hundred-mile journey he took with his disciple Sora.

After Bashō 's death in 1694, appreciation of his work continued to grow. His work has been translated into many languages, and readers around the world admire his observations of the natural world in keen and concise verse. Haiku remains one of the most popular poetic forms in the world, and Bashō is still the most famous poet of Japan's Edo period.

Gwendolyn Brooks (1917 – 2000)

As far as poets go, Gwendolyn Brooks is real cool. She was born in Kansas, but her family moved to Chicago soon after. By the time she was sixteen, more than seventy of her poems had been published. Her first book of poems, *A Street in Bronzeville*, published in 1945, exemplified the kind of rhythm, rhyme, and lyrical genius that she would become known for. Five years later, she became the first African American to win a Pulitzer Prize in poetry, for her collection *Annie Allen*. Like much of her work, the poems in *Annie Allen* deal with social issues of the urban poor, in particular African-American women. Raised in a very socially aware family, Brooks was always sensitive to and interested in writing, lyrically, about the struggles and triumphs of children and families in the Chicago community. This interest, along with her stature as a poet, led her to become the literary mother of Black Arts poets like Nikki Giovanni and Haki Madhubuti.

Gwendolyn Brooks published twenty volumes of poetry; a novel, *Maud Martha;* two autobiographies; and two books for children. She was also the Poet Laureate of Illinois and the first

African-American woman to be appointed Consultant in Poetry to the Library of Congress. The Gwendolyn Brooks Cultural Center at Western Illinois University and a middle school in Harvey, Illinois, were named in her honor.

Sandra Cisneros (b. 1954)

Novelist, poet, and short-story writer Sandra Cisneros was born in Chicago and grew up in a family with six brothers. They spent much of their childhood moving between Chicago and Mexico. Cisneros's literary style is very spare and lyrical, not only in her poetry but in her prose as well. She often incorporates Spanish words into her work, when they more precisely convey meaning or improve the rhythm of a particular passage.

While best known for her novel *The House on Mango Street* (1984), which won an American Book Award from the Before Columbus Foundation, she is also the author of several books of distinguished poetry. A National Endowment for the Arts Fellow, a MacArthur Fellow, and a devoted community activist, Cisneros uses her writing to explore Chicana identity and the challenges of being immersed in Mexican and Anglo-American cultures simultaneously.

Billy Collins (b. 1941)

New York City native Billy Collins has been called "the most popular poet in America" by the *New York Times*. His use of simple everyday language often employs wit and humor and frequently explores familiar and mundane subjects like eating breakfast cereal or making a cup of tea, which explains his reputation for accessibility in his poetry. He served one term as New York State Poet Laureate and two terms as U.S. Poet Laureate. As U.S. Poet Laureate, Collins edited *Poetry 180*, a collection of poems to be read to high-school students over the 180 days of the school year. The poems are available online free of charge and have become a part of many high-school ELA curriculums.

Billy Collins is the author of fourteen collections of poetry, as well as a children's book called *Voyage*. Among his many honors, Collins received the Poetry Foundation's Mark Twain Award for Humor in Poetry, a National Endowment for the Arts Fellowship, and a Guggenheim Fellowship. He taught writing and literature for more than thirty years at Lehman College in New York. He continues to teach and conduct readings all over the world. Most recently, Collins served as Senior Distinguished Fellow of the Rollins Winter Park Institute in Florida. He also speaks regularly on National Public Radio.

e. e. cummings (1894–1962)

Edward Estlin Cummings was born in Cambridge, Massachusetts, at the end of the nineteenth century. He decided to become a poet when he was still a little boy, and from the ages of eight to twenty-two, he wrote a poem a day. He graduated from Harvard University, and early selections of his poems were published in 1917 in *Eight Harvard Poets*, a collection of poems by Harvard Poetry Society members. During the First World War, he served as a volunteer ambulance driver in France. He was arrested and held in prison for suspicion of espionage, an experience he fictionalized in his novel, *The Enormous Room*. A year after his release, he was drafted into the U.S. Army and spent half a year in a training camp.

His first book of poetry, *Tulips and Chimneys*, was published in 1923. Cummings took the rules of poetry and the conventions of English and turned them inside out. His poetry is often described as a kind of literary cubism, with cut-up lines arranged purposefully on the page. Cummings also used the typewriter as tool, taking advantage of the machine's spacing and symbol keys to enhance his verse with visual elements. Although his writing technique is unique, the topics of his poems are often traditional themes such as childhood or love. He published many more collections of poems, as well as a play called *Him*, and *EIMI*, a travel diary. Cummings died in 1962, at the height of his popularity. More than fifty years later, he remains one of the most admired modern American poets.

Emily Dickinson (1830–1886)

Though Emily Dickinson is today considered an extraordinary and well-known poet, only a handful of her poems were published during her lifetime. She grew up in Amherst, Massachusetts, and lived out her life in her father's home there. Dickinson never married and ventured out rarely; instead, like Henry David Thoreau, she simplified her life as much as possible. She had a rich interior life, built on the powers of her imagination.

Her poems began on scraps of paper such as used envelopes or on the backs of recipes, which she carried around in her pockets. Consequently, the objects and materials described in her poems are conventional things like flowers, robins, and ordinary household items. But there is nothing ordinary about Emily Dickinson's poems, which are innovative in terms of syntax, punctuation, and rhyme.

Her language is elliptical, and her unique poems are known for their precision and wit. Her poetry contains references to the Bible, the works of Shakespeare, classic mythology, and contemporary hymns. After her death, forty hand-bound volumes of poetry were discovered in the bottom drawer of her bureau. She wrote nearly two thousand poems; none are titled, and none are longer than fifty lines.

Robert Frost (1874 – 1963)

No twentieth-century American poet was more revered in his lifetime than Robert Frost. Widely read and honored repeatedly, Frost was the country's unofficial poet laureate for many years. Poems such as "Stopping by Woods on a Snowy Evening," "The Road Not Taken," "Birches," and "Mending Wall" are American classics. Though he is often associated with New England, Robert Frost was born in San Francisco in 1874. His family later moved to Massachusetts to live with his grandfather after his father died. His first published poem, "My Butterfly," appeared in 1894, but he struggled initially as a poet and worked as a poultry farmer and a teacher. Frost moved to England with his family in 1912, and his first two books, *A Boy's Will* and *North of Boston,* were published during his time there. By the time he returned to the United States, his literary reputation had grown considerably.

His lyrical poems are renowned for their brilliant craftsmanship and flawless rhyme and meter. He once famously compared writing free verse to playing tennis without a net. Frost's poems were almost always set in the New England countryside, and the familiar natural images and use of ordinary American speech made his work accessible to the masses, but the underlying themes in his work are often far more serious. Four of his six children died, and Frost wrote about grief, loneliness, and life's fragility in ways that continue to resonate with readers.

In 1924, Frost won his first of four Pulitzer Prizes. He was a popular reader and toured the country giving talks and reading his poems. Although he attended both Dartmouth and Harvard, he never graduated from college. (Both colleges eventually awarded him honorary degrees.) He taught at many of the country's leading colleges, including Harvard and Dartmouth, as well as Amherst, Middlebury, and the University of Michigan. As America's most-read poet, he recited his poem, "The Gift Outright" at the inauguration of President John F. Kennedy in 1961.

Chief Dan George, OC (1899 – 1981)

Chief Dan George was born in North Vancouver under the name of Geswanouth Slahoot. His surname was changed to George when he entered school at the age of five. Before becoming the chief of the Tsleil-Waututh Nation, he worked as a construction laborer, a longshoreman, and a school-bus driver. He began an acting career in 1960 and received numerous awards, including an Academy Award nomination, for his performance in the film *Little Big Man.*

At a celebration for Canada's centennial, he delivered his solemn speech, "Lament for Confederation," which begins, "Today, when you celebrate your hundred years, oh Canada, I am sad for all the Indian people throughout the land." In 1971, he was named an Officer of the Order of Canada (OC). His best-known written collection, *My Heart Soars,* was published in 1974. Part of the title poem was read by actor Donald Sutherland at the opening ceremony of the 2010 Olympics in Vancouver. Chief Dan George is remembered as a powerful voice for native peoples.

Nikki Giovanni (b. 1943)

Yolanda Cornelia "Nikki" Giovanni Jr. grew up in Lincoln Heights, Ohio, but spent many summers in Knoxville, Tennessee, where she was born. It was those summers with her grandparents that fostered an ear for and a lifelong love of storytelling. During the 1960s Giovanni attended Fisk University in Nashville; the university was undergoing an African-American cultural renaissance at the time, and as editor of the campus literary magazine, she was part of that. With the publication of her first book of poetry, *Black Feeling, Black Talk,* Giovanni became one of the leading voices of the Black Arts movement. Her first three books of poetry were successful and helped create a large audience for her work. Her poetry expresses a pride in African-American culture, as well as love for family and friends. Nikki Giovanni is the author of more than fifteen books of poetry and a dozen children's books. She has taught at a number of colleges and universities, including Virginia Tech, Ohio State, and Rutgers.

Giovanni's work is notable for its wonderful use of metaphor and simile, its attention to history and contemporary culture, and its fiery energy and wit. Her strong sense of the oral tradition of poetry along with her frankness and natural charisma have made her a popular poet throughout the United States. She has received numerous honors and awards for her work, including the City College of New York Langston Hughes Award, the Rosa Parks Women of Courage Award, three NAACP Image Awards for Literature, a National Book Award Finalist selection, a National Association of Radio and Television Announcers Award for Best Spoken Word Album, and more than twenty honorary degrees.

Terrance Hayes (b. 1971)

Terrance Hayes was an Academic All-American basketball player at Coker College, in his home state of South Carolina. In his last year there, he decided to pursue poetry and switched his major from studio art to English. His professors encouraged him to apply to graduate school, and he received his MFA from the University of Pittsburgh in 1997.

Since the publication of his first book of poetry, *Muscular Music* (1999), Hayes has won numerous awards, including a Push-cart Prize and fellowships from the National Endowment for the Arts, the Guggenheim Foundation, and the MacArthur Foundation. His second book of poems, *Hip Logic* (2002), was chosen for the National Poetry Series, and his collection *Lighthead* (2010) won a National Book Award. His newest book, *How to Be Drawn*, was published in 2015.

Hayes taught at Carnegie Mellon University for twelve years and has been a professor of English at the University of Pittsburgh since 2013. His poetry reflects on his experiences as an African-American man, and he addresses controversial subjects with honesty, humor, and a musical, playful use of language. He often experiments with different forms to heighten the impact of his messages, and his poems are filled with references to jazz and popular culture.

Langston Hughes (1902–1967)

Born in Joplin, Missouri, Langston Hughes started writing poetry when he was just thirteen. Hughes was raised by his grandmother. She was the widow of Lewis Sheridan Leary, who participated in John Brown's raid on Harper's Ferry—a failed attempt to create an insurrection that would free the slaves in the American South. Hughes attended Columbia University to study engineering, but left after one year to work on a ship headed to Europe and pursue his writing. He traveled throughout his life and held many jobs before establishing himself as a writer.

His first published poem, "The Negro Speaks of Rivers," remains one of his most popular. His first collection of poetry, *The Weary Blues,* was published in 1926, and his first novel, *Not Without Laughter,* was released in 1930. His poems were deeply influenced by blues, jazz, and African spirituals, often incorporating the sounds and rhythms of these genres. Much of his writing, including the famous poem "Mother to Son," also imitates natural speech patterns. This quality gives Hughes's work an intimacy that resonates with readers.

As the "poet laureate of the Harlem Renaissance," Hughes was a powerful voice for the black community, bringing attention to the rich culture and achievements of African Americans through his writing, as well as speaking out against racism. Black life in America from the 1920s to the 1960s was his subject, and no one reflected the day-to-day lives of ordinary people, their woes and wonders, the way he could. Hughes had an optimistic vision for the future and an undying hope in humanity that never left him.

Incredibly prolific, Hughes published fifteen collections of poems, two novels, nine short-story collections, opera librettos, autobiographies, essays, plays, radio and televisions scripts, a number of children's books, and some translations.

Walter Dean Myers (1937–2014)

Award-winning author Walter Dean Myers was born in Martins-burg, West Virginia. After the death of his mother while she was giving birth to his sister, his father, George, sent Walter to Harlem to live with his first wife and her husband, Florence and Herbert Dean. Walter later adopted the middle name Dean in their honor. When he was very young, his mom, who couldn't read very well, read with him in the afternoons. Myers struggled in school and suffered from a speech impediment, but he loved to read and this soon transformed into a love of writing. He dropped out of high school and joined the army; years later, while working construction, he remembered the sage advice of one of his high-school teachers, who told him to keep on writing no matter what. His break as an author came after he won a contest for his entry entitled *Where Does the Day Go?*

Renowned for his young adult novels, including the award-winning *Monster* and *Somewhere in the Darkness*, Myers was also a prolific poet, often composing autobiographical poems that chronicled the goings-on in his Harlem community. Sharon Creech used Myers's poem "Love That Boy," as the basis of her award-winning novel in verse *Love That Dog*. Throughout his career, Myers advocated for cultural diversity and a broader range of experiences to be reflected in books for children, and he often wrote about his own difficult teenage years.

Over a span of forty-five years, Myers wrote more than a hundred books for children and teenagers. He received numerous honors, including two Newbery Honors, five Coretta Scott King Author Awards, and six Coretta Scott King Author Honors. Three of his books were chosen as National Book Award Finalists. In 2012, he was named the National Ambassador for Young People's Literature.

Pablo Neruda (1904–1973)

The Chilean poet known as Pablo Neruda was born Neftalí Ricardo Reyes Basoalto. He had already won several literary competitions by the time he completed high school. In 1923, he sold all his possessions to finance the publication of his first collection, *Crepusculario (Twilight),* under his pseudonym, due to his family's disapproval of his occupation as a writer. After his acclaimed cycle of love poems titled *Veinte poemas de amor y una canción desesperada (Twenty Love Poems and a Song of Despair),* was published to great success in 1924, Neruda decided to give up his studies and write full-time. These poems were passion-filled and established his poetic tradition of equating women with nature, which continued throughout his lifetime. Decades later, he wrote *Los versos del Capitán (The Captain's Verses)*, a collection of intense love poems about his third wife, Matilde Urrutia.

There was a longstanding tradition in Latin America of sending writers overseas to serve as diplomats, and Pablo Neruda was no exception. He served as honorary consul to Rangoon, Burma, starting in 1927, and in the 1930s he served as Chilean consul to Spain. He was there in 1936, when the Spanish Civil War broke out, and the violence that he witnessed there deeply affected him and influenced his writing. His support of the Republican cause cost him his position, although he later served in diplomatic posts in France and Mexico. Neruda became internationally known with his two-volume collection of poems, *Residencia en la tierra (Residence on Earth)*. The powerful poems in these books are a despairing look at the larger problems of human existence. Poems in subsequent collections often called for social change and were political in nature.

Throughout his life, Neruda participated in politics and acted as a social commentator in addition to his writing. The passion he brought to his political life was fueled by the same level of intensity that characterizes his famous love poems. He was a fervent communist, and his political activism led him to seek exile in Mexico from 1948 to 1952. Upon his return to Chile, his poetry became less political and more focused on the wonders of the natural world. In 1970, he was nominated for president on the Chilean Communist Party ticket. He published dozens of collections of poems and in 1971 was awarded the Nobel Prize for Literature.

Whether love sonnets or tributes to political heroes, Pablo Neruda's poems were anchored in the imagery found in his beloved homeland. He is admired for the depth and beauty of his language, and his love poetry is cherished for its dreamlike quality, rich with metaphors and similes.

Naomi Shihab Nye (b. 1952)

Naomi Shihab Nye was born in St. Louis, Missouri. Her father was a Palestinian refugee, and her mother was American. Much of her work is influenced by her experiences with different cultures. Her poems often celebrate ordinary things and people she encounters every day. Her first full-length collection of poems, *Hugging the Jukebox* (1982), celebrates diversity and connection. Her perspective is at once worldly and anthropological yet down to earth. Her third volume of poems, *Fuel* (1998), is highly acclaimed and admired for its sense of moral urgency about international issues.

After the 9/11 attacks, Nye spoke out against both terrorism and prejudice. Her book *19 Varieties of Gazelle: Poems of the Middle East* (2002) is a collection of poems about her experiences as an Arab-American. Her next collection, *You & Yours* (2005), explores the Middle East in personal ways. She has published nine more poetry collections since then, and has also edited several poetry anthologies and written fiction, songs, and poetry for children, as well as a young adult novel, *Habibi* (1997). Her highly acclaimed children's book *Sitti's Secrets* (1994) concerns an Arab-American child's relationship with her grandmother living in a Palestinian village.

Naomi Shihab Nye has won numerous awards and fellowships, including four Pushcart Prizes, the Jane Addams Children's Book Award, the Paterson Poetry Prize, American Library Association Best Book and Notable Book citations, and the Robert Creeley Award. She was named laureate of the NSK Neustadt Prize for Children's Literature in 2012. Her body of work is marked by its sensitivity, cross-cultural awareness, and humanity.

Mary Oliver (b. 1935)

Born in Ohio, Mary Oliver spent most of her adult years in Provincetown, Massachusetts, on Cape Cod, and many of her beloved poems are rooted in this landscape. Both her poems and prose celebrate the natural world with precision and a universality that transcends the specifics and speaks to readers of all ages. Oliver has been called our greatest living nature poet, as well as America's best-selling poet. She is a poet of careful observation, with a keen ability to articulate the wisdom and wonder found in the natural world. There is a deep spirituality in her poems that honors the English Romantic poetic tradition. Oliver's poems about animals are particularly popular with young people, and her books are filled with poems with titles such as "Owls," "Toad," "Porcupine," "Turtle," "The Kitten," and "The Opossum."

Her work spans decades and includes more than twenty-five collections of poetry, as well as a half dozen books of prose. Her books on craft, *A Poetry Handbook* and *Rules for the Dance,* are very popular. She has received numerous literary awards, including the Pulitzer Prize for Poetry in 1984 for her collection *American Primitive* and a National Book Award in 1992 for *New and Selected Poems*. She is the recipient of a Guggenheim Fellowship, a Christopher Award, an American Academy of Arts and Letters Award, a Lannan Literary Award, and a Shelley Memorial Award.

Okot p'Bitek (1931 – 1982)

Okot p'Bitek was a Ugandan poet, playwright, and novelist who gained international acclaim with the English-language publication in 1966 of *Song of Lawino,* a long narrative poem about a rural

African wife whose discontented husband is always wishing that their life were more modern and westernized. His second book of poems, *Song of Ocol* (1970), is the husband's response to the wife's lament in *Song of Lawino*. His third book of poems, *Two Songs*, was published in 1971. These three collections are considered to be some of the finest African poetry in print. An activist and scholar in African tradition and religion, p'Bitek was also a master storyteller. His poetry is epic, often centering on Acholi culture, the image of African women, and liberation from colonialism.

Born in the North Uganda grasslands, p'Bitek was educated at Gulu High School, then King's College, Budo. At school he was noted as a singer, dancer, drummer, and soccer player. He went on to study education at the University of Bristol, law at the University of Wales, Aberystwyth, and then social anthropology at the University of Oxford. He served as director of Uganda's National Theatre from 1966 to 1968. During the terrifying and repressive decade when dictator Idi Amin held control of Uganda (1971–1979), p'Bitek taught at several universities outside the country.

Rumi (1207 – 1273)

Rumi was born at the start of the thirteenth century to Persian-speaking parents in Balkh, now part of Afghanistan. His family later relocated to Konya, in modern-day Turkey, to evade a Mongol invasion. Rumi was a scholar and a teacher until, at age thirty-seven, he met Shams of Tabriz, a dervish who had taken a vow of poverty. Rumi's friendship with Shams began his transformation into a mystic poet. Three years later, Shams mysteriously disappeared, and Rumi poured his grief into the composition of lyric poetry. His remains the largest body of lyric poetry in the Persian language. Rumi composed more than forty thousand lyric verses in a variety of styles. His work is deeply spiritual and inspirational and can still be heard recited in churches, synagogues, and mosques around the world today. It is the kind of poetry people might copy onto a piece of paper to carry around in a pocket. Coleman Barks, the foremost translator of Rumi's works into English, has been a driving force in keeping the ancient poet's work relevant and accessible.

William Carlos Williams (1883 – 1963)

William Carlos Williams grew up in Rutherford, New Jersey. His father loved literature, particularly Shakespeare, and his mother was a painter. While attending Horace Mann High School in New York City, he decided to become both a doctor and a writer. During his first year of college at the University of Pennsylvania,

Williams met Ezra Pound. Pound introduced him to the poet H.D. (Hilda Doolittle), and together they formed the imagist movement, which called for a break from formulaic poetry. Their poems were free-verse poems built out of precise images.

Williams established his medical practice in 1910, and he wrote poems and practiced medicine in Rutherford for the next forty years. Inspired by the world of his patients, he wrote on prescription pads and between patient visits. He explored new forms of poetry that were completely unique by experimenting with meter and enjambment (the continuation of a single thought from one line to another). Williams wanted his poems to mimic the American language that he heard in everyday conversations.

He is the author of more than twenty books, including novels; volumes of poetry, short stories, and essays; an opera libretto; and an autobiography. *Paterson,* considered Williams's epic and an American masterpiece, is a poem that comprises five volumes and the fragment of a sixth. Set in Paterson, New Jersey, it is marked by Williams's innovative approach to breaking lines called the variable foot. Williams was awarded the first National Book Award for poetry. His last book of poems, *Pictures from Brueghel,* won the Pulitzer Prize in 1963; he died the same year.

Judith Wright (1915 – 2000)

Australian poet Judith Wright was born in New South Wales and studied English, philosophy, and psychology at the University of Sydney. Following the Second World War, her first book of poetry, *The Moving Image,* was published while she was working as a research officer at the University of Queensland. In 1950, Wright moved to Tambourine Mountain with novelist Jack McKinney. They married in 1962. After Jack's death in 1966, she moved to Braidwood, New South Wales. Deeply influenced by the Braidwood Highlands and her years on Tambourine Mountain, Wright's work became more focused on the natural world. She is remembered now not only for her writing but also for heightening awareness of environmental destruction and Aboriginal land rights. She is the author of more than twenty books of poems and literary criticism as well as a number of nonfiction books about environmental issues.

ANCIENT AND FOREIGN-LANGUAGE POETS

Bashō (Japan)
Rumi (Persia)

NINETEENTH-CENTURY POETS

Emily Dickinson (United States)

TWENTIETH-CENTURY POETS

Gwendolyn Brooks (United States)
e. e. cummings (United States)
Robert Frost (United States)
Chief Dan George (Canada)
Langston Hughes (United States)
Pablo Neruda (Chile)
Okot p'Bitek (Uganda)
William Carlos Williams (United States)
Judith Wright (Australia)

CONTEMPORARY POETS

Maya Angelou (United States)
Sandra Cisneros (United States)
Billy Collins (United States)
Nikki Giovanni (United States)
Terrance Hayes (United States)
Walter Dean Myers (United States)
Naomi Shihab Nye (United States)
Mary Oliver (United States)

ABOUT THE CREATORS

KWAME ALEXANDER is a poet, educator, and *New York Times* best-selling author of thirty-five books, including *Becoming Muhammad Ali*, coauthored with James Patterson; *Rebound*, which was short-listed for the Carnegie Medal; *The Undefeated*, illustrated by Kadir Nelson, which won the Caldecott Medal and received a Newbery Honor; and the Newbery Medal–winning middle-grade novel *The Crossover*. A regular contributor to NPR's *Morning Edition*, he is the recipient of numerous awards and honors, including the Lee Bennett Hopkins Poetry Award, a Coretta Scott King Author Honor, three NAACP Image Award nominations, and the inaugural Conroy Legacy Award. In 2018, he opened the Barbara E. Alexander Memorial Library and Health Clinic in Ghana as a part of LEAP for Ghana, an international literacy program he cofounded.

CHRIS COLDERLEY is a poet and elementary school teacher in Burlington, Ontario. His articles and poems have appeared in *Language Magazine*; *California English*; *Inscribed*; *Möbius, The Poetry Magazine*; *Maple Tree Literary Supplement*; *Teach*; and *Tower Poetry*.

MARJORY WENTWORTH is a former Poet Laureate of South Carolina. Her books of poetry include *Noticing Eden*, *Despite Gravity*, and *The Endless Repetition of an Ordinary Miracle*, and she has authored, cowritten, and coedited many other titles. She teaches at the Art Institute of Charleston, and her work is included in the South Carolina Poetry Archives at Furman University.

EKUA HOLMES is a fine artist who has devoted her practice to sustaining contemporary Black art traditions in Boston. She has received numerous awards, both for her artworks and in recognition of her community outreach and curatorial efforts. She won a Coretta Scott King Illustrator Award for her illustrations in *The Stuff of Stars* by Marion Dane Bauer, and she received a Caldecott Honor and a John Steptoe New Talent Illustrator Award for her illustrations in *Voice of Freedom: Fannie Lou Hamer, Spirit of the Civil Rights Movement* by Carole Boston Weatherford. Ekua Holmes lives in Boston.

For Nikki and Ginney
K. A.

To Danielle, Bill, and Marge for believing at the times I do not
C. C.

To Joshua Caleb Lance Douglas
M. W.

For Song, my beautiful granddaughter
who brings love and laughter wherever she goes
E. H.

Preface copyright © 2017 by Kwame Alexander
Poems copyright © 2017 by the individual authors
Illustrations copyright © 2017 by Ekua Holmes

First paperback edition 2021

Originally published as *Out of Wonder: Poems Celebrating Poets*, Candlewick Press 2017.

Library of Congress Catalog Card Number 2017931505
ISBN 978-0-7636-8094-7 (hardcover)
ISBN 978-1-5362-2194-7 (paperback)

21 22 23 24 25 26 CCP 10 9 8 7 6 5 4 3

Printed in Shenzhen, Guangdong, China

This book was typeset in Myriad.
The illustrations were done in collage on paper.

Candlewick Press
99 Dover Street
Somerville, Massachusetts 02144

visit us at www.candlewick.com